Library of
Davidson College

MANAGEMENT
OF AMERICA'S
NATIONAL DEFENSE

Library of
Davidson College

The Francis Boyer Lectures on Public Policy

MANAGEMENT OF AMERICA'S NATIONAL DEFENSE

David Packard

American Enterprise Institute for Public Policy Research

Distributed by arrangement with

UPA, Inc.
4720 Boston Way
Lanham, MD 20706
3 Henrietta Street
London WC2E 8LU, England

ISBN 0-8447-1383-X

Library of Congress Catalog Card Number 87-070086

©1987 by the American Enterprise Institute for Public Policy Research, Washington, D.C. All rights reserved. No part of this publication may be used or reproduced in any manner whatsoever without permission in writing from the American Enterprise Institute except in the case of brief quotations embodied in news articles, critical articles, or reviews.

The views expressed in the publications of the American Enterprise Institute are those of the authors and do not necessarily reflect the views of the staff, advisory panels, officers, or trustees of AEI.

"American Enterprise Institute" and ⓐ are registered service marks of the American Enterprise Institute for Public Policy Research.

Printed in the United States of America

American Enterprise Institute
1150 Seventeenth Street, N.W., Washington, D.C. 20036

THE
FRANCIS BOYER LECTURES
ON PUBLIC POLICY

The American Enterprise Institute initiated the Francis Boyer Lectures on Public Policy in 1976 to examine the relationship between business and government in American society. The lectures are made possible by an endowment from the SmithKline Beckman Corporation in memory of Mr. Francis Boyer (1893–1972), the late chairman of the board of the corporation and a distinguished business leader for many decades.

The lecture is given annually, by an eminent thinker who has developed notable insights on the relationship between the nation's private and public sectors. It is intended to illuminate central issues of public policy in contemporary America and contribute significantly to the dialogue by which the public interest is served.

The American Enterprise Institute's distinguished Council of Academic Advisers selects the Francis Boyer lecturer. The lectureship carries an award and stipend of $10,000. Lecturers may come from any walk of life—the academy, the humanities, public service, science, finance, the media, business, or industry. The man or woman delivering the lecture is not necessarily a professional scholar, government official, or business leader. The principal considerations determining the selection are the quality and appositeness of the lecturer's thought rather than his or her formal qualifications.

The Francis Boyer Lecture is delivered in Washington, D.C., before an invited audience, at the conclusion of the American Enterprise Institute's year-end Public Policy Week. These several days of seminars bring together government policy makers, business leaders, and scholars for the purpose of exploring some of the policy problems facing the United States and the world.

David Packard, the 1986 Francis Boyer Award recipient, was chosen in recognition of his many contributions to American business, technology, and government. Mr. Packard's lecture, *Management of America's National Defense*, explores ways to improve this large, complex administrative task. His important contribution to the defense management debate is likely to help achieve more efficient administration in an era when budgetary constraints are forcing difficult policy choices yet our world has not, alas, become a less dangerous place. It is a topic for which Mr. Packard is superbly equipped by intellect and experience. His familiarity with problems of defense management and his keen interest in them derive from his long and spectacularly successful business career at the Hewlett-Packard Company (of which he is now chairman of the board); from his service as deputy secretary of defense from 1969 to 1971; and from his chairmanship of the President's Blue Ribbon Commission on Defense Management from 1985 to 1986. Many of that commission's recommendations, as well as some of those set forth in this Francis Boyer Lecture, are currently being implemented.

The American Enterprise Institute is very pleased to

publish David Packard's *Management of America's National Defense* as part of the Francis Boyer Lectures on Public Policy.

CHRISTOPHER C. DEMUTH
President
American Enterprise Institute

Francis Boyer Award Recipients

1977   The Honorable Gerald R. Ford
1978   The Honorable Arthur F. Burns
1979   Paul Johnson
1980   William J. Baroody, Sr.
1981   The Honorable Henry A. Kissinger
1982   Hanna Holborn Gray
1983   Sir Alan Walters
1984   The Honorable Robert H. Bork
1985   The Honorable Jeane J. Kirkpatrick
1986   The Honorable David Packard

COUNCIL OF ACADEMIC ADVISERS OF THE AMERICAN ENTERPRISE INSTITUTE

D. GALE JOHNSON, Chairman, *Eliakim Hastings Moore Distinguished Service Professor of Economics and Chairman, Department of Economics, University of Chicago*

DONALD C. HELLMAN, *Professor of Political Science and International Studies, University of Washington*

ROBERT A. NISBET, *Adjunct Scholar, American Enterprise Institute*

HERBERT STEIN, *A. Willis Robertson Professor of Economics Emeritus, University of Virginia*

MURRAY L. WEIDENBAUM, *Mallinckrodt Distinguished University Professor and Director, Center for the Study of American Business, Washington University*

JAMES Q. WILSON, *Henry Lee Shattuck Professor of Government, Harvard University*

Introduction

As AEI's chairman I have the distinct pleasure and great honor to introduce to you the man whom our Council of Academic Advisers has selected to deliver this year's Francis Boyer Lecture. I think everyone is aware that Francis Boyer was the chairman of SmithKlein Beckman and was tremendously interested in public policy formulation.

The man chosen by our council is none other than Mr. David Packard, and I cannot think of a more deserving and more distinguished lecturer than David Packard. Not only is he the cofounder of one of our great technological companies, Hewlett-Packard, which he and Bill Hewlett founded in 1939, but also he has had a distinguished record in public service: as deputy secretary of defense and as chairman of the Commission on Defense Management, which is better known to all of us as the Packard Commission.

He happens to be the first trustee of the American Enterprise Institute who has been selected to deliver this lecture. He was not selected because he is a trustee, but he is particularly near and dear to our heart. He has been a loyal and devoted member of the board of AEI because he believes that it is a national treasure. And all I can say to you in introducing David Packard is that I join the Council of Academic Advisers in saying to you, he is a national treasure.

WILLARD C. BUTCHER
Chairman, AEI Board of Trustees

At the end of June this year, the President's Blue Ribbon Commission on Defense Management completed its work with its final report to President Reagan. Since that time legislation to reorganize the Office of the Joint Chiefs of Staff (JCS) consistent with our recommendations has been enacted by the Congress and signed by the president.

Legislation to establish a new under secretary position in the Department of Defense, which the commission recommended, to provide for a full-time professional manager for the defense acquisition process has been enacted. A well-qualified man has been appointed and is already hard at work in the Pentagon.

This is good progress in improving defense management, but it is only a small beginning on the job that needs to be done. Further progress will depend on continuing involvement on the part of those people and those organizations actively interested in improving defense management. It is for this reason that I decided to review tonight the recommendations of the commission. We need your help in making further progress on this important issue.

I know that many of you here are familiar with the recommendations of the commission. For those who are, I want to refresh your memories; for those who are not I believe it is important for you to know about our recommendations. I am sure the recommendations we have made are not the optimum; some probably should be modified, some may be wrong. For this reason continued public discussion is important. It is in the interest of everyone in this country who seeks peace and freedom in this troubled world to keep our American military capability strong. We have not been using our resources very well in doing this important job. I am very sure we will get much more military capability for the billions of dollars we are spending if the recommendations of this commission are effectively implemented.

In our interim report, given to the president February 28, 1986, we separated our recommendations into four major areas: national security planning and budgeting, military organization and command, acquisition organization and procedures, and government-industry accountability. Let me stress that none of these recommendations stands alone—they are intended to work together as a package, and they were arrived at with considerable thought and deliberation as to how one will affect the others.

The major objective of this country's defense management must be to plan sensibly for an uncertain future, to answer new and unexpected threats to our security, and to make the best use of our technological and industrial capabilities and resources. And one of the most serious problems in our defense management process has its roots in the way planning and budgeting are done.

We say in the interim report, today there is no rational system whereby the executive branch and the Congress reach coherent and enduring agreement on national military strategy, the forces to carry it out, and the funding that should be provided—in light of the overall economy and competing claims on national resources. The absence of such a system contributes substantially to the instability and uncertainty that plague our defense program.

Better long-range planning must be based on military advice of an order not now always available—fiscally constrained, forward looking, and fully integrated. This advice must incorporate the best possible assessment of our overall military posture vis-à-vis potential opponents and must candidly evaluate the performance and readiness of the individual services and the unified and specified commands.

To conduct such planning requires a sharpened focus on major defense missions in the department's presentation, and Congress's review, of the defense budget. The present method of budget review, involving duplicative effort by numerous congressional committees and subcommittees, centers on either the minutiae of line items or the gross dollar allocation to defense and obscures important matters of strategy, operational concepts, and key defense issues.

To deal with this problem the commission made a number of recommendations relating to the organization and the responsibilities of the Office of the Joint Chiefs of Staff. In making these recommendations, the commission had two objectives in mind. The first was to improve the command of the U.S. military forces deployed around the world under the unified commanders, including both the established worldwide commands and those assigned for specific actions, such as Lebanon and Grenada. Second, the commission's recommendations were designed to give the chairman of the joint chiefs and the unified commanders a stronger role in the process of deciding what new weapons should be acquired and in distributing the resources available among the military departments.

The specific changes recommended were the following. Current law should be changed to designate the chairman of the joint chiefs of staff as the principal uniformed military adviser to the president, the National Security Council, and the secretary of defense, representing his own views as well as the corporate views of the JCS.

Current laws should be changed to place the joint staff and the organization of the joint chiefs of staff under the exclusive direction of the chairman, to perform such duties as he prescribes. The service chiefs should continue to serve as members of the JCS. The chairman would not need their concurrence in supporting his recommendations to the president and the secretary of defense. The position of a four-star vice chairman should be established by law as a sixth member of the JCS. The vice chairman should assist the chairman by representing the interests of the unified commanders, cochairing the Joint Requirements Management Board, and performing such other duties as the chairman may prescribe.

Subject to the review and approval of the secretary of defense, unified commanders should be given broader authority to structure subordinate commands, joint task forces, and support activities in a way that best supports their missions and results in a significant reduction in the size and numbers of military headquarters. Legislation to make these changes has been enacted, and they are being implemented by the DoD.

With these changes in place we strongly recommend that the president give the secretary of defense five-year budget guidance. This would take defense planning off the year-by-year basis that has been the practice since

1958, when the last major legislation on Defense Department organization was enacted.

The commission's second report dealt with the acquisition process. The president established the commission in part because public confidence in the effectiveness of the defense acquisition system has been shaken by a spate of "horror stories"—overpriced spare parts, test deficiencies, and cost and schedule overruns. Unwelcome at any time, such stories are particularly unsettling when the administration and Congress are seeking ways to deal with record budget deficits.

We analyzed the horror stories, as others have done, but concluded that a diagnosis based on recognized deficiencies could lead only to band-aid treatments for a system more fundamentally ill. Therefore, our basic methodology was deliberately quite different.

We compared the defense acquisition system with other systems, both government and commercial, that develop and produce equipment of comparable complexity, in order to find success stories that could provide a model on which reforms of the defense acquisition system could be based. Defense acquisition is the largest and, in our judgment, the most important business enterprise in the world. It deserves to be managed with the highest standards. We therefore conducted a "search for excellence" by examining organizations that had been most successful in acquisition, in order to find a model of excellence for defense acquisition.

The major recommendations on acquisition were presented in our report issued in April, a formula for action. We identified six underlying features that typified the most successful commercial programs and that could be incorporated in the defense acquisition system:

- *Clear command channels.* A commercial program manager has clear responsibility for his program, and a short, unambiguous chain of command to his chief executive officer (CEO), group general manager, or some comparable decision maker.
- *Stability.* At the outset of a commercial program, a program manager enters into a fundamental agreement or "contract" with his CEO on specifics of performance, schedule, and cost. So long as a program manager lives by this contract, his CEO provides strong management support throughout the life of the program. This gives a program manager maximum incentive to make realistic estimates and maximum support in achieving them.
- *Limited reporting requirements.* A commercial program manager reports only to his CEO. Typically, he does so on a "management-by-exception" basis, focusing on deviations from plan.
- *Small, high-quality staffs.* Generally, commercial program management staffs are much smaller than in typical defense programs, but personnel are hand-selected by the program manager and are of very high quality. Program staff spend their time managing the program, not selling it or defending it.
- *Communications with users.* A commercial program manager establishes a dialogue with the customer, or user, at the conception of the program when the initial trade-offs are made and maintains that communication throughout the program. Generally, when developmental problems arise, performance trade-offs are made—with the user's concurrence—in order to protect cost and schedule. As a result, a program manager is motivated to seek out

and address problems, rather than hide them.
• *Prototyping and testing*. In commercial programs, a system (or critical subsystem) involving unproven technology is realized in prototype hardware and tested under simulated operational conditions before final design approval or authorization for production.

It is clear that defense acquisition typically differs from this commercial model in almost every respect. Yet a number of successful DoD programs have incorporated some or all of these management features to a greater or lesser degree. We therefore concentrated our efforts on deriving a formula for action—steps by which defense acquisition can come to emulate this model to the maximum extent practical.

To improve the acquisition process, the commission made the following recommendations:

• We strongly recommended creation by statute of the new position of under secretary of defense (acquisition) and authorization of an additional Level II appointment in the Office of the Secretary of Defense (OSD). This new under secretary should have full-time responsibility for managing the defense acquisition system. As I said earlier, this position has been established by legislation, and this new under secretary is already hard at work in the Pentagon.

• Another important recommendation was to make better use of technology to reduce cost and improve performance. We recommended a high priority on building and testing prototype systems to demonstrate that new technology can substantially improve military capability and to provide a basis for realistic cost estimates prior to a full-scale development decision.

- In order to obtain a better balance between cost and performance, we recommended that a restructured Joint Requirements and Management Board (JRMB), cochaired by the under secretary of defense (acquisition) and the vice chairman of the joint chiefs of staff, should play an active and important role in all joint programs and in all major service programs. The JRMB should define weapon requirements for development and provide thereby an early trade-off between cost and performance.

The commission noted that substantial savings could result from more stability in major acquisition programs and that expanded use of commercial products could save literally billions of dollars.

Our third report, "National Security Planning and Budgeting," was issued in June. It describes in detail how the president should provide the five-year budget guidance and how the reorganized JCS should develop an overall military strategy and plan the force structure to support the strategy.

The work behind the report confirmed that the new planning process we recommend can be done with existing procedures. We recommended that this new planning process be utilized in preparing the two-year defense budget for FY1988 and 1989.

Our fourth report, "Conduct and Accountability," deals with the increasingly troubled relationship between the defense industry and the government. Our report notes that from its earliest days, the United States has relied on private industry for procurement of needed military equipment. The vigor of industry is indispensable to the successful defense of America and the security of our people.

The Department of Defense annually conducts business with some 60,000 prime contractors and hundreds of thousands of other suppliers and subcontractors. In 1985, the department placed contracts worth approximately $164 billion, 70 percent of which went to a group of 100 contractors. Twenty-five contractors did business of $1 billion or more, 147 did $100 million or more, and almost 6,000 did $1 million or more.

Acquisition of the tools of defense is an immense and complex enterprise. The commission believes that DoD reliance on private industry has not been misplaced. The success of this enterprise, however, is now clouded by repeated allegations of fraudulent industry activity. With notable results, DoD has devoted increased attention and resources to detecting and preventing unlawful practices affecting defense contracts. But a plethora of departmental auditors and other overseers—and the burgeoning directives pertaining to procurement—also have tended to establish a dysfunctional and adversarial relationship between DoD and its contractors.

Widely publicized investigations and prosecutions of large defense contractors have fostered an impression of widespread lawlessness, fueling popular mistrust of the integrity of the defense industry. A national public opinion survey, conducted for the commission in January 1986, revealed that many Americans believe defense contractors customarily place profits above legal and ethical responsibilities. The following specific conclusions can be drawn from this survey:

Americans consider waste and fraud in defense spending a very serious national problem and one of major proportions. On average, the public believes almost half the defense budget is lost to waste and fraud. Four in five Americans think that defense contractors should feel an obligation, when doing business with DoD, to observe ethical standards higher than those observed in their normal business practices.

The depth of public mistrust of defense contracting is deeply disquieting for a number of reasons. First, the public is almost certainly mistaken about the extent of corruption in industry and waste in the department. While fraud constitutes a serious problem, it is not as extensive or costly as many Americans believe. The nation's defense programs lose far more to inefficiency than to dishonesty.

Second, a lack of confidence in defense contractors may affect public support for important defense programs and thus weaken our national security. Restoring public confidence in our acquisition system is essential if we are to ensure our defense.

Third, the current popular impression of runaway fraud and waste undermines crucial support for implementing precisely those management reforms that would increase efficiency. These include executive and congressional support for sensible new longer-term planning and budgeting procedures, recommended by the commission, to eliminate major but hidden costs that instability imposes on our overall defense efforts.

Fourth, the commission is concerned that the current adversarial atmosphere will harm our industrial base. It is important that innovative companies find it desirable to contract with DoD. In current circumstances, important companies could decide to forgo this opportunity.

Finally, it is significant that private businesses bear the brunt of public indignation over waste and fraud in our defense programs. With most Americans, we believe that those who contract in the defense of our country must perform at a higher level than business as usual. It stands repeating, from our interim report, that:

> Management and employees of companies that contract with the Defense Department assume unique and compelling obligations to the people of our armed forces, the American taxpayer, and our nation. They must apply (and be perceived as applying) the highest standards of business ethics and conduct.

By this measure, the national opinion survey represents a striking vote of no confidence in defense contractors generally.

Though government oversight is critically important to the acquisition process, no conceivable number of additional federal auditors, inspectors, investigators, and prosecutors can police it fully, much less make it work more effectively. Nor have criminal sanctions historically proved to be a reliable tool for ensuring contractor compliance. We conclude there is a particular urgency in dealing affirmatively with contractor practices.

To this end, leaders in the defense industry recently have committed themselves to an initiative, consistent with recommendations of our interim report on government-industry accountability, that promises collective and highly constructive action. This noteworthy effort is embodied in a document signed to date by at least thirty-two major defense contractors who pledge to adopt and to implement a set of principles of business ethics and conduct that acknowledge and address their corporate responsibilities under federal procurement laws and to the public. All signatories pledge to:

- have and adhere to written codes of conduct
- train their employees in such codes
- encourage employees to report violations of such codes, without fear of retribution
- monitor compliance with laws incident to defense procurement
- adopt procedures for voluntary disclosure of violations and for necessary corrective action
- share with other firms their methods for and experience in implementing such principles, through annual participation in an industry-wide "best practices forum"
- have outside or nonemployee members of their boards of directors review compliance

I am greatly encouraged by this voluntary initiative on the part of the defense industry to deal with this serious problem. It will take time and continued effort, but in the end I am convinced that the relationship between government and the defense industry will improve.

I want to conclude with some general observations about the work of the commission.

First, and very important, our observations and recommendations should not be taken as criticism of the present administration of the DoD. The problems were there long before Secretary Weinberger took charge. In fact, he had already begun to deal successfully with many of them.

Secretary Weinberger has added impressive strength to our military capability. The defense budget is 50 percent higher in constant dollars than it was in 1980. In my letter to the president accompanying our interim report I said,

At the outset of our work we recognized the substantial progress made in the last five years to improve the nation's defense. The morale and fighting ability of our armed forces are higher than at any time in recent memory.

The recommendations of the commission will bring only limited benefits unless a better spirit of teamwork can be developed among the participants—the OSD, the services, the administration, and, particularly, the Congress. In the past it has required a major international crisis to bring about good teamwork, particularly from the Congress.

Even modest improvements in defense management can bring significant benefits in better military capability at lower cost, and continuing public interest can help bring this about.

I appreciate the opportunity AEI has given me to deliver this message. I hope all of you will continue to support the work of our commission.